The Heart
of Suffolk

IN OLD PHOTOGRAPHS

The Heart of Suffolk

IN OLD PHOTOGRAPHS

Collected by
HUMPHREY PHELPS

Alan Sutton Publishing Limited
Phoenix Mill · Far Thrupp
Stroud · Gloucestershire

British Library Cataloguing in Publication
Data

Phelps, Humphrey
Heart of Suffolk in Old Photographs
I. Title
942.64

ISBN 0-7509-0431-3

Typeset in 9/10 Sabon.
Typesetting and origination by
Alan Sutton Publishing Limited.
Printed in Great Britain by
Redwood Books, Trowbridge.

First published 1993

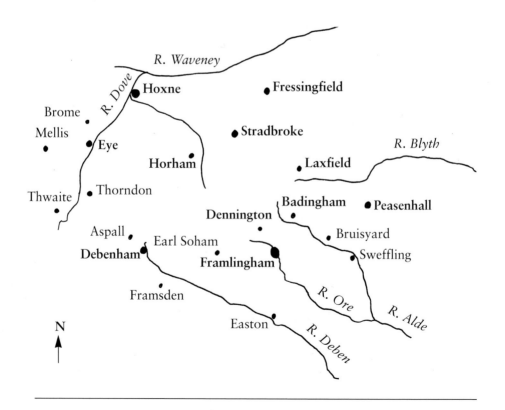

Contents

Introduction

The parishes covered by this book have been the dairying district of Suffolk since the seventeenth century. In 1874 a French visitor, François de la Rochefoucauld, observed that the countryside was 'superb' and that the area around Framlingham 'had the best cows in all England for giving milk'. Immense quantities of butter were produced in the localities of Framlingham, Debenham, Eye and Stradbroke and conveyed to London markets by road wagons.

Enclosure, completed by the mid-nineteenth century, brought change, as well as distress, to many. Even Arthur Young, the first Secretary to the Board of Agriculture and an advocate of enclosure, was moved to say that by nineteen enclosure Bills out of twenty the poor were injured and given nothing but the workhouse.

Looking at these photographs today it is easy for us to become nostalgic and regret the passing of 'the good old days'. There was much good in those days and much to regret in their passing. But we should bear in mind that as well as the good there was much hardship, and fear of the workhouse hung over many for the greater part of the period covered by this book.

The photographs were taken during the very last years of the nineteenth century and the first half of this century. Most of them date from 1900 onwards, but to understand even the latest ones we cannot overlook the nineteenth century. Many depict scenes which are still well within living memory, yet nearly all have more affinity with the nineteenth century than they have with today. They depict an era far more remote than the number of years suggest.

The nineteenth century saw a great improvement in the system of farming – the introduction of the Norfolk Four Course Rotation and what was known as 'High Farming'. Until the mid-twentieth century farming was dominant throughout the whole district. The majority of men worked on the land or at some trade connected, directly or indirectly, with the land. (The biggest industry was the manufacture of corn drills.) Rural population increased until the middle of the nineteenth century, but then began to decrease. The prolonged agricultural depression which started in 1879 hastened the exodus to the town and this continued.

However, in 1900 it was still a busy countryside, with men and horses working in the fields. Farming was the bedrock of the economy, even if that bedrock was rather shaky, and the horse was the pivot of the farm. Scores of craftsmen were busy in the small towns and villages; windmills and watermills were still turning. (Every parish had at least one windmill and some had watermills too.) Communities were self-contained. The muscle of local men and home-bred horses was the major source of power on the farms. The local bootmakers shod the men and the local blacksmiths shod the horses. The local tailors made clothes and the local saddlers made the harness. Village wheelwrights made the wagons and the parish mills ground the corn. These craftsmen and tradesmen, together with an abundance of shopkeepers, supplied the necessities of life. And the money went round and round the district just as the windmill sails went round and round in the wind. It was a system we may well envy.

By 1937 the number and variety of trades had diminished, but many were still in existence where there are none today. I could not help comparing the scenes in the photographs with the same scenes in more recent times. Framlingham, Debenham and Eye are all still charming places but none has the vitality of that era which was not so long ago. In the photographs there are many men working in the fields, and even in the 1950s gangs of them could still be seen. But not anymore. In 1901 there were over 27,000 farmworkers in Suffolk, but by 1981 there were fewer than 5,000. Not even the Black Death depopulated the rural landscape as modern farming has done. The horses and the men have quit the fields, the craftsmen their benches. The centuries-old rural structure has been destroyed. When we look at these photographs and at the same places today we are looking at different worlds. But distance in time and the camera are powerful enchanters.

The photographs in the book are grouped more or less thematically, and no attempt has been made to arrange them in chronological order. The first seven sections are topographical, making a circular tour in a clockwise direction which starts at Framlingham and ends at Dennington. The next section is a similar tour but this time is concerned solely with schools. Then comes a section on farming – a large section for obvious reasons. And, finally, there is a section on people which is the largest of all because the study of people is the most interesting subject. And these sons and daughters of the Heart of Suffolk are worth studying. Their roots went deep into their native soil, they spoke in their native and delightful accent, they worked together and for each other and made their own amusements. Oh, the days that they saw which are no more!

I am a lover of Suffolk but not a native, and compiling this book has been a great pleasure. It has, in fact, afforded me several pleasures, the principal one being meeting those people whose generosity and help have made the book possible. To them I express my gratitude, with the hope that the book meets with their approval.

SECTION ONE

Framlingham

Framlingham, the finest small town in East Suffolk.
Julian Tennyson

Celebrations at Market Hall.

Trades	1844	1937
Bakers	6	3
Blacksmiths	3	–
Bootmakers	17	1
Braziers and Tinners	2	–
Brewers	2	–
Butchers	5	5
Cabinet Makers	5	–
Corn Merchants	3	1
Cornmillers	3	1
Curriers and Dyers	4	–
Farmers	30	31
Glovers	2	–
Grocers and Drapers	5	9
Inns and Taverns	6	8
Ironmongers	4	4
Joiners/Carpenters	7	2
Maltsters	3	–
Milliners	13	–
Saddlers	2	3
Straw Hat Makers	4	–
Tailors	12	3
Wheelwrights	4	1

Old House and Castle, *c.* 1900. During her short stay at this, one of the chief baronial castles, Mary Tudor was proclaimed Queen before being taken to London. The stone in the right hand corner is covering the well.

Bridge Street, *c.* 1910.

Church Street, *c.* 1900. Richard Green, author of *A History of Framlingham* (1834), lived in this street.

Filling the water cart at Pump Spring, *c.* 1900. The town had a number of wells, but water was also drawn from ponds and rivers.

Filling a water cart from the pump (which is behind the horse), early 1900s. In 1938 the District Council started supplying water from a pumping station, and in January 1938 Frank Baldry, builder and plumber, was offering to connect water to households.

Scotch Greys at Market Hill, early 1900s.

Fire damage in Fore Street, August 1905. A candle set fire to some curtains in one house, the fire engine was hampered by a lack of water, and five houses were destroyed.

Water was not lacking on 26 August 1912. The Mere and Castle seen from New Road.

The flood at Albert Place, 26 August 1912. Damant's the post office and newsagents is on the right, and Mr Robinson is driving through the water.

Another view of the same flood. A. Bonney's bakery is on the left and Damant's is on the right. Ironically, there is a pump in the foreground! (Photograph by John Self)

J. Scoggins' shop at 24 Well-Close-Square, 1920s.

J. Scoggins' billhead,
1906.

A. Bonney, the Albert bakery, 1908.

Billhead of Edwin G. Clarke & Son, maltsters, 1907.

Mount Pleasant Mill or Buttons Mill, *c.* 1900. This post-mill, the whole body of which turned to face the wind, was one of two mills at this site. This one originally stood at Apsey Green. In the background, centre, is a weather vane, the owner of which prepared weather forecasts in the nineteenth century.

Victoria Mill was a tower mill, where only the cap revolved to face the wind. In 1881 a storm blew the sails off; new ones were fitted later. The mill was demolished in 1962. A timber-built mill stood on this site until 1842.

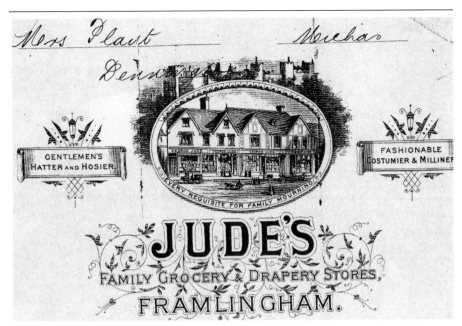

Jude's billhead (1905), a Market Hill grocery and drapery store. Grocery and drapery were often combined in one business.

Jarvis Scoggins' shop, 24 Well-Close-Square, in the nineteenth century.

WASH DAYS MADE EASY
BY USING A SUFFOLK MANGLE

PRICES from 27/6

  AND GUARANTEED

We hold a stock of RUBBER

WRINGERS from 12/11

including the famous

ACME WRINGERS from 39/-

 CASH OR EASY TERMS ARRANGED

  DELIVERED FREE

Advertisement in the *Framlingham Weekly News*, 1 January 1938.

The 'Fram Flyer', taking on coal, *c.* 1950. The Wickham Market to Framlingham line opened in 1859. On the day the first train arrived at Framlingham the church bells rang throughout the day. Passenger service ended during 1952 and the line finally closed in 1965.

The Framlingham line. This was a special train laid on to bring boys back to Framlingham College. There is a sign on the front of the engine. (Photograph by Dr Ian Allen of Framlingham)

The tanyard which was owned by Frank Read, who also had a leather-cutting shop in Fore Street. The tanner turned hides into leather.

The Hamilton Harriers in Market Hill, 28 February 1906. In 1872 the 10th Duke of Hamilton brought a famous pack of harriers and kennelled them at Easton.

Suffolk Horses at the Framlingham Show. The show dates from 1893 or even a little earlier. Today it is a horse show, but until the 1930s it was a general livestock show.

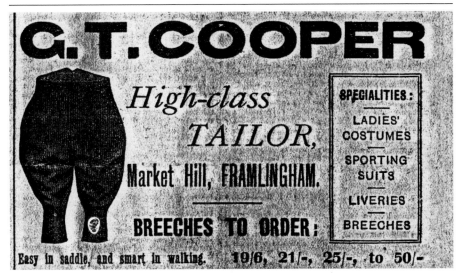

Advertisement in the *Framlingham Weekly News*, 15 December 1906.

Well-Close-Square, *c*. 1900. On the left is J. Scoggins' shop, while John Self's tailors shop is centre. (Photograph by John Self)

H.E. Singleton, general supply stores and post office at Sweffling.

Post-mill at Earl Soham.

Easton. The estate at Easton formerly belonged to the Earls of Rochford and then to the Duke of Hamilton, who also had large estates in Scotland.

Easton village. In the nineteenth century the parish had a cooper, wheelwright, blacksmith, tailor, grocer and draper, two shoemakers and a hedge carpenter.

The Mansion, Easton.

The Mansion, Easton, the seat of the Earl of Rochford, who thoroughly repaired it prior to his death in 1830. It then passed to the Duke of Hamilton who rarely 'sat' here. It was taken down in 1920 and shipped to America where it was rebuilt.

Gale damage at Easton, 12 April 1909.

SECTION TWO

Debenham

Debenham is as beautiful a little Suffolk town as you will find.
John Seymour

High Street, *c.* 1900.

Trades	1844	1937
Bakers	1	2
Basket Makers	–	1
Blacksmiths	4	–
Beer Houses	3	–
Bootmakers	11	–
Butchers	3	2
Cabinet Makers	2	–
Corn Millers	3	–
Curriers	2	–
Farmers	12	15
Glovers	3	–
Grocers and Drapers	5	4
Inns and Taverns	4	4
Ironmongers	1	–
Joiners/Carpenters	5	2
Maltsters	2	–
Milliners	3	–
Saddlers	3	1
Straw Hat Makers	2	–
Tailors	7	4
Tinners & Braziers	1	–
Wheelwrights	2	–

High Street, looking towards the church of St Mary. In 1932 the church battlement was taken down and reset, and four bells recast. A tumbril (left) and a steam engine (centre) can be seen in the photograph. Note the gas lamps – the town was lit by gas from 1858.

High Street in the early 1900s. On the left is Baldry Brothers' store.

High Street, 1950s.

The flood in August 1957.

Another view of the flood in 1957.

Delivery boy, early 1900s.

The school, 1940s. A school was 'called into existence' at Debenham in 1653 by Cromwell. From its foundation onwards 'it did little to maintain a reputation for grammar teaching'. In 1866 the Commissioners described it as 'non-classical' and ranked with 'a somewhat inferior National School'.

Post-mill at Framsden. Mr Webster (right), miller, and Dick Read with one of the five butchers carts belonging to F.E. Neave of Debenham.

Page's post-mill, Kenton Road, Debenham, 1904. This mill had cloth sails.

Tower mill, Gracechurch Street.

Gracechurch Street, early 1900s.

The Foresters Hall (left), which was built in 1905 with seating for 600 people. The Foresters was a Friendly Society and very small weekly payments entitled its members to sickness benefits. In Debenham the Society had a branch called 'The Star of Suffolk', and in 1911 it was one of the largest branches with over 1100 members.

The Cherry Tree Inn. In 1845 the following encroachments were noted on Cherry Tree Green: three cottages and their gardens, an iron foundry, the National School (built 1834), and an osier bed. By 1845 the Horse and Lamb Fair, formerly held on this green, had to be held on a field behind the Cherry Tree Inn.

F.E. Neave & Son's butchers cart in front of the Saddler's Shop, 1930s.

The Saddler's Shop, *c*. 1900 or earlier, belonging to Mr Rumsey, seen here wearing a bowler hat. The small boy (left) was the last Rumsey to own the shop. Leonard Aldous, who started with Lionel Rumsey in 1913, eventually took over the business. In 1844 there were over 140 saddlers in Suffolk. In the 1930s the greatest demand was for farm harness. Horse collar making called for especial skill.

Tolgate Corner.

Getting clay ready for brickmaking at Pug Mill. As the clay went into the mill water was pumped over it. The clay came out in a liquid form and the water had to be drained. The clay in block form then went to the brickmakers, who put it in moulds. During the winter brickmaking was discontinued.

Fire damage at the Paint Shop, 1911.

Hammond's hawkers' van at Debenham, *c.* 1920. The hawker supplied many household necessities. On the side of the van are frails, enamel mugs, buckets, plates, cups and jugs, brushes and broom heads, and hand-bowls. And there would be many more utensils inside, with oil or paraffin at the rear. The boy is holding an oil measure.

Mr List's Debenham Horse Omnibus, early 1900s.

F.E. Neave & Son's butchers shop, *c.* 1950. This butcher specialized in Suffolk-cured bacon and ham. The hams, after soaking in brine, are put in a black treacly solution and after some weeks are removed and smoked. The cure takes about ten weeks in all. Suffolk-cured bacon and ham can still be obtained from these premises. Dennis Smith (left) and Henry Woods are in front of the shop.

Debenham church bells, which were cast in 1761 and rehung on ball-bearings in 1932. On 18 October 1890 a peal of 5,040 Bob Triples was rung. On 3 December 1890, 5,056 Superlative Surprises were rung in three hours two minutes.

Suffolk Cider display at Aspall Hall, 1920s (since when the spelling has been changed to 'cyder'). Cider making was started in Aspall Hall in 1728 by Clement Chevalier, who came from Jersey. He planted orchards and imported a granite wheel from the Isles de Chaussée for the cider mill. The cost of transport was £6. The wheel, pulled by a horse, was in use until 1947. The orchards at Aspall are managed by organic methods and cyder is still made here. In 1819 another member of the family, the Revd Mr Chevalier, raised a famous variety of barley, known as Chevalier, from a single ear selected by a farmworker. By the end of the century 90 per cent of barley grown in England was Chevalier. It was still in cultivation fifty years later before being succeeded by more modern varieties.

SECTION THREE

Eye

Eye is a beautiful little place.

William Cobbett

Church Street, *c*. 1900. On the left is the Eight Bells, selling Adnams Southwold Ale and Stout.

Trades	1844	1937
Agricultural	–	1
Implement Makers	1	
Bakers	5	2
Basket Makers	1	–
Beer Houses	7	–
Blacksmiths	4	2
Bootmakers	6	1
Brewers	2	1
Butchers	4	3
Coopers	1	–
Corn Dealers	1	2
Farmers	28	22
Grocers and Drapers	9	9
Inns and Taverns	12	8
Ironmongers	3	1
Joiners/Carpenters	6	1
Maltsters	1	1
Millers	3	1
Milliners	4	–
Saddlers	3	–
Straw Hat Makers	2	–
Tailors	6	1
Tinners and Braziers	2	–
Wheelwrights	2	1

The thatched cottage, castle and church in Castle Street, early 1900s. The castle was built by William Mallet of Normandy, one of William the Conqueror's men at the Battle of Hastings. He died fighting Hereward the Wake.

Castle Street from a similar viewpoint on 26 March 1906. William Cobbett visited Eye on 17 March 1830 and said it was 'a beautiful place though an exceedingly rotten borough' and a 'fertile and thickly-populated neighbourhood'. In the evening he lectured at 'the neat little playhouse'. The theatre was built in 1815 and opened on 18 June 1815, the day of the Battle of Waterloo.

Broad Street, late 1890s. The Kerrison Memorial was erected in 1888 to the memory of Sir E.C. Kerrison Bart (1821–86), MP for Eye 1852–86. Eye returned two members to Parliament until the Reform Act of 1832.

Broad Street, 1905. The ironmongers can be seen rear right. A corn market and a cattle sale were held on Mondays in the town. Eventually Eye lost its markets to Diss.

Beale Brothers, Broad Street, showing the interior of the ironmongers shop. The staircase was removed in the mid-1980s.

Another view of the interior of the ironmongers.

Ruined house in Magdalen Street. In the eighteenth century Eye gained some prosperity from manufacturing lace, but this affluence gradually declined during the nineteenth century.

Magdalen Street, 1912.

Castle Street, 1911. Stayer House, formerly 'Fetchetts', was once the home of the D'Eye family. At one time it was owned by the flax-master.

Church Street, 1912. The rent of Harwen House provided a charity: 50s each Christmas to 'poor widows and maidens of Eye'.

Station Road.

Lambseth Street, site of the old rettery. The flaxworks gave employment to a couple of hundred people until it was destroyed by fire in 1864. A pump in the street drew water from the river for the water carts, which sprayed the streets when they became dusty.

Eye railway station, Magdalen Street. Eye was the terminus of the Mellis and Eye line. The railway to Norwich (1849) missed Eye by several miles, to the detriment of Eye, and hastened the town's decline.

Mellis railway station, 1908. The Mellis to Eye branch line was one of the shortest branch lines in England. It was opened in 1867 and was locally owned until taken over by the Great Eastern Railway at the end of the nineteenth century. The line did little to stem the decline of Eye. It was closed to passenger traffic in 1932, but continued with freight until 1964.

Castle Street. Stanley House, which was built in the seventeenth century, is in this street. At one time it was a private school.

The White Lion Hotel. Lettering over the archway into the yard proclaims 'Posting Establishment'. The boys in the carriages, off on an outing, are from the Kerrison Approved School, Thorndon, founded in 1856.

The White Lion yard was an old coaching inn composed of Tudor buildings. On one side of the yard there was a ballroom with a musicians' gallery and an Adam fireplace. In the nineteenth century, after a County Yeomanry demonstration, the White Lion provided a dinner at 2s 6d per head, including 'as much wine and punch as each man could swallow'. Most regrettably this splendid inn was closed a few years ago.

An Eastern Counties Omnibus at Eye.

Possibly the Red Lion yard, Church Street. It is likely that Mr and Mrs J. Keer are in the gig as 'J. Keer' is on the sign on the side of the gig.

The Ipswich to Norwich Road, *c.* 1900, viewed from Twaite Buckshead near Brockford, Braiseworth.

Cranley post-mill (just outside Eye). The miller, Mr Woods, is standing at the door with his daughter, Dorothy. This mill was partly constructed from material from the mill which stood on Eye Castle Mound from before 1690 until the nineteenth century. An oil painting of that mill, by J.S. Cotman, is in the Castle Museum at Norwich. A post-mill once stood on a site near the hospital. Races used to be held on Cranley Green in July and lasted for two days.

SECTION FOUR

Hoxne and Fressingfield

Hoxne, a quiet, delightful village built up and down a valley.
Julian Tennyson

R. Wilcox's bakers van, the Hygienic Steam Bakery, Hoxne.

Trades	1844	1937

HOXNE

Trades	1844	1937
Bakers	1	–
Beer Houses	1	–
Blacksmiths	4	1
Bootmakers	4	–
Butchers	1	1
Carpenters	1	1
Corn Millers	1	–
Farmers	25	31
Grocers and Drapers	4	4
Inns	3	1
Linen Manufacturers	1	–
Saddlers	1	–
Tailors	1	–
Wheelwrights	1	1

FRESSINGFIELD

Trades	1844	1937
Bakers	1	–
Beer Houses	3	–
Blacksmiths	3	1
Bootmakers	2	1
Butchers	2	1
Corn Millers	2	1
Farmers	44	46
Glovers	1	–
Grocers and Drapers	3	3
Inns	3	4
Joiners/Carpenters	2	–
Saddlers	1	–
Straw Hat Makers	1	–
Tailors	2	–
Wheelwrights	2	1

Low Street, *c.* 1900. Beneath the trees is the village pump, and the sixteenth-century St Christopher public house is behind the trees. Cheapjacks sold their wares on the green and held singing and dancing competitions. Eventually the trees became unsafe and were felled.

The village pump in Low Street, 26 October 1923. The police station is behind the pump. The pump was later converted into a seat and moved to a more central position on the green.

The Red Lion Inn, Hoxne, was one of the six public houses that once served the village. Low-timbered ceilings were a feature of the building, which was destroyed by fire in 1964.

Hoxne watermill, on the River Waveney, was built on the site of an older watermill. In 1900 it was owned and worked by Mr Chase, who is standing by the sluice-gate. The rowing boat was for hire. The mill ceased working after the Second World War.

Hoxne post-mill, *c.* 1920, stood on high ground above the watermill and was the last mill to work in Hoxne. It was demolished in the 1920s.

The back of the churchyard and the Old Guildhall at Fressingfield. The church has some fine fifteenth-century bench-ends, and the initials A.P. on a bench are those of Alice de la Pole, a granddaughter of Chaucer.

The Fox and Goose Inn, originally the Guildhall, Fressingfield, 1905. At one time the upper floor was a schoolroom.

The Angel Inn, Fressingfield, which closed in around 1960.

The Stores, Fressingfield, *c*. 1925.

Church Street, Fressingfield, early 1900s.

Church Hill, Fressingfield.

Fressingfield, once known as 'Merry Fressingfield', early 1900s.

The churchyard and vicarage, Fressingfield, 1906. Dr William Sancroft, Archbishop of Canterbury in the seventeenth century, was born at Ufford Hall in this parish, where he resided after sacrificing his high office because of his conscientious scruples. He is buried in the churchyard.

Fressingfield's fire engine, 1914. The men are, left to right: Bob Etheridge, Mr Ridley, Jumbo Vinson, Herbert Etheridge, Mr Dowson, Mr Etheridge, Nutty Barber, Dr James, Harry Harper.

Fressingfield post office, 1915. The postman is Mr Carter.

Post-mill, Mill Ground, Fressingfield, which was demolished around 1940. Fressingfield also had two more windmills.

Stradbroke and Horham

Stradbroke is a pretty little place.

John Seymour

All Saints church, early 1900s. The whole building was completely repaired and refurnished in 1872.

Trades	1844	1937

STRADBROKE

Bakers	3	1
Basket Makers	1	–
Beer Houses	3	–
Blacksmiths	7	1
Bookbinders	1	–
Bootmakers	8	–
Braziers and Tinners	1	–
Brewers	1	–
Butchers	3	3
Cabinet Makers	1	–
Coopers	1	–
Corn Millers	3	–
Farmers	39	39
Gig Makers	1	–
Glovers	1	–
Grocers and Drapers	5	3
Inns	2	4
Joiners	3	–
Linen Manufacturers	2	–
Maltsters	1	–
Milliners	3	–
Saddlers	3	1
Tailors	3	–
Wheelwrights	5	–

HORHAM

Agricultural Implement Makers	1	–
Blacksmiths	2	1
Drapers	1	1
Farmers	12	10
Grocers	1	–
Inns	1	1
Millers	1	1
Shoemakers	2	–
Shoekeepers	1	2
Wheelwrights	2	1

The church bells. The church has one of Suffolk's six rings of ten bells. The earliest bell dates from the fifteenth century, the latest two were made in 1952.

New Street. Five outlying greens were enclosed in the early nineteenth century, but are still called greens.

Diss Road, 1906.

Diss Road under snow.

Queen Street, 1906. In 1854 local farmers built a Corn Hall, at a cost of £550, which is now the library.

Queen Street, 1908, named after the Queen's Head. The building dates from the seventeenth century and has a Victorian front.

Church Street, 1904.

The school, early 1900s. A document of 1862 stated that the new school was intended for the children of the labouring poor of the parish, but not the inmates of the workhouse, and that parents should be members of the Church of England.

The Reading Room and tennis players, 1910.

The Fancy Fair.

Skinners Mill, Stradbroke, a post-mill with a fantail which turned the sails to face the wind. A roundhouse is beneath the buck.

The Four Cross Ways, Horham.

Stradbroke Road, Horham, 1913.

Low Road, Horham.

The Dragon Inn, Horham.

SECTION SIX

Laxfield and Peasenhall

Peasenhall, where they make the best drills.

Adrian Bell

Laxfield post office, 1900.

Trades	1844	1937
LAXFIELD		
Bakers	1	1
Beer Houses	3	–
Blacksmiths	2	1
Bootmakers	6	1
Butchers	1	1
Corn Millers	2	1
Curriers	1	–
Farmers	34	30
Grocers and Drapers	3	3
Inns	4	4
Maltsters	–	1
Saddlers	2	–
Tailors	3	–
Wheelwrights and Carpenters	6	2
PEASENHALL		
Bakers	1	1
Blacksmiths	3	1
Bootmakers	5	2
Butchers	3	1
Coopers	1	–
Corn Millers	1	1
Drill Manufacturers	1	1
Farmers	18	17
Grocers and Drapers	2	3
Inns	2	1
Joiners	2	–
Saddlers	1	–
Tailors	1	–
Wheelwrights	3	–

General stores and post office, Laxfield, 1914. John Noyes, a Laxfield shoemaker, was burned at the stake in Queen Mary's reign for his religious beliefs. Taken before the Bishop of Norwich, he refused to recant and was taken back to Laxfield and burnt.

William Reeves' butchers shop, Laxfield, *c.* 1905. A Christmas display.

Putting a tyre on a wheel, Laxfield. The iron tyre has to be heated and expanded to fit on to the wheel. Water is then poured on the tyre to cool it and to shrink it, ensuring a tight fit.

The back of the Guildhall at Laxfield. The Guildhall was first recorded in 1461 as a 'cherchehous' for use as a religious and charitable guild. Later it was used to house poor people. Today it is a museum.

Post-mill, Laxfield, *c*. 1907.

Post-mill, Laxfield.

The Mid-Suffolk Light Railway, Laxfield station. The Haughley to Laxfield line opened in 1908, but a goods service started in 1904. The distance between the two stations was nineteen miles. There was a crowd of cheering people to see the first passenger train leave Laxfield, and about thirty detonators were exploded to enliven the event.

Laxfield station in the 1930s. The line closed in 1952 and the building (left) went to Bedfield. The closed Haughley to Laxfield line was the setting for John Hadfield's delightful novel *Love on a Branch Line*.

Badingham children boarding the last train from Laxfield on 28 July 1952.

The Street, Peasenhall, *c.* 1900. First on the left is Emmett's Stores, noted for its Suffolk-cured ham and bacon. On the right is the stream-cum-drain which runs through the village.

Providence House, Peasenhall, 1902. This is where Rose Harsent worked and lived-in until she was murdered one night in 1902.

Peasenhall, early 1900s. Julian Tennyson, author of *Suffolk Scene*, lived at Peasenhall.

The drill works of James Smyth & Sons Ltd. The works were adjacent to the church at Peasenhall. Here, the famous Suffolk or Peasenhall Drill was developed. James Smyth put his first drill on the market in 1800 and the firm continued to make drills until the works closed in 1965. One drill, bought in 1830, was in use until 1964.

Blacksmith's shop at Peasenhall, early 1900s. Mr Rodwell, the blacksmith, is standing in the doorway.

Harness shop, The Street, Peasenhall, *c.* 1930. Mr Newsome, the harness maker, is at the doorway with two horse collars beside him.

Mr Hunt, a cooper, at work in his shop in Bruisyard Road, Peasenhall.

SECTION SEVEN

Badingham and Dennington

Dennington, a large and pleasant village.
White's Directory, 1844

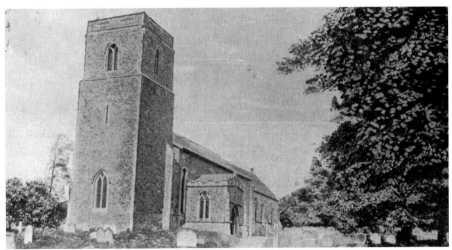

Badingham church. William Dowsing, appointed Parliamentary Visitor to the Churches of Suffolk in 1643 with the job of destroying superstitious ornaments etc., smashed sixteen 'cherubims' belonging to this church.

Trades	1844	1937
BADINGHAM		
Beer Houses	2	–
Blacksmiths	1	1
Bootmakers	2	–
Carpenters	2	2
Corn Millers	2	–
Farmers	27	25
Grocers and Drapers	4	3
Inns	1	2
Tailors	1	–
Wheelwrights	2	1
DENNINGTON		
Basket Makers	–	1
Beer Houses	1	–
Blacksmiths	2	1
Bootmakers	3	1
Butchers	1	–
Carpenters	1	–
Corn Millers	2	–
Farmers	11	23
Grocers and Drapers	3	1
Tailors	3	–
Wheelwrights	1	–

Low Street, Badingham. The school is at the far end.

Low Street, Badingham. On the right is A.H. Watson, general stores, next to the old school.

The school, Low Street, Badingham. It is now the village hall.

The Hamilton Harriers at Colston Hall, 1930s.

Post-mill, either at Mill Road or Badingham.

Oakenhill Hall, Bruisyard. This is 'Crackenhill Hall' of *Joseph and his Brethren*. This fine rural novel, which has a good claim to be the best of all rural novels, was written by H.W. Freeman and first published in 1928. Set in Bruisyard it is authentic in detail and to read it is like living and working with Joseph and his brethren.

Red Polls at Bruisyard. Until the 1960s this Suffolk breed was a familiar sight in the county.

The church of St Mary, Dennington, 1963. The church contains a monument to Lord Bardolph, who fought at Agincourt, was Captain of Harfleur, Governor of Calais, and treasurer of the household of Henry V. The church has a fine Reformation canopy of a hanging pyx over the high altar, probably the only one existing in England; one of the bench-ends, the Sciapus, is the only known example of this subject.

Bob Reeve, sexton, sitting at the sand table at Dennington church, 1890s. The sand table was used to teach children to write.

The post office, Dennington, *c.* 1900. There has been a post office on these premises since 1830, a record which no, or hardly any, other building can rival. The first official post from Framlingham was established at Dennington in May 1845. The Baldry family held these premises for about 200 years.

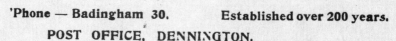

'Phone — Badingham 30.   Established over 200 years.

POST OFFICE, DENNINGTON.

11th March .... 19~~3~~50

Robert, Dennington Parish Counc

Dr. to ...

Wm. J. Baldry & Sons.

Boot and Shoe Makers, Stationers, ~~Ironmongers~~ &c.

Agents for the "ROYAL" Fire Insurance Co. Ltd ,

and Employers' Liability Assurance Corporation, Ltd.,

At the back of the post office the Baldrys had a bootmaking and repair shop.

Arthur Daines' basket making shop at Dennington. Mr Daines is standing outside. He was a regular supplier of horse-feeding skeps to the royal family at Sandringham. Apart from white willows, all willows were grown locally. When Arthur Daines died in 1954, he was succeeded by his son Jack and daughter Nellie. The shop closed in 1970.

The Queen's Head, Dennington, *c.* 1900. The Queen's Head still has a thatched roof in this photograph, but it was tiled in the early 1900s. Records for the building date back to 1483. In the last century, when harvest was done, local farmers gave a largesse (harvest supper) to their men and families. Ale was then 2s a gallon.

The Queen's Head in the late nineteenth century, with carriages on 'the village green'. Until the early years of this century rent days at Michaelmas were held here and farmers came to pay their rents. Here bread and coals were also distributed to the poor by the Charity Trustees.

The Square, Dennington, 1906, with the village shop in the background. An East Suffolk Police Force was formed in 1840.

The village stores, 1965. The shop closed on Christmas Eve 1989.

Fire at Dennington, *c.* 1913.

The Mill House, Badingham Road, Dennington. Owned by George Saunders, it was a working mill until the late 1920s. It was then bought by Arthur Daines, the basket maker, who pulled it down. Spare parts from the demolished mill went to repair other mills in the locality.

Bought of G. W. M. SAUNDERS

—◦▷◦ MILLER, &c. ◦◁◦—

G.W.M. Saunders' billhead.

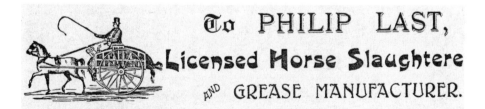

To PHILIP LAST,
Licensed Horse Slaughtere
AND GREASE MANUFACTURER.

Philip Last's billhead. Philip Last of the White House slaughtered horses when they became too old or ill to work. He then sold them as dog meat or grease. Some of the latter was sold to grease the stiff, heavy leather boots which all land workers then wore. Some of the former no doubt fed the local hunt's foxhounds.

The hunt at Red House Farm, Dennington, in the early 1920s. In the photograph are Miss Cook, Miss Cook, Bob Nesling MFH, Mr Stephenson, Miss Beryl Leman (the girl with the hounds).

The Square, Dennington, 1947. The Annual British Legion Drawing Match, during which 386 furrows were drawn by the competitors, seventeen of whom were women. The match was held on land owned by Major Pryor and A.H. Mann. Awards went to: 1. Hubert Taylor, 2. Royden Chenery, 3. Oscar Chenery. Third from left, with trilby and moustache, is James Wardley.

SECTION EIGHT

Schools

Learning is most excellent.

Anon

The chemical laboratory, Eye Grammar School, 1915.

The college, Framlingham, was established in 1864 as a memorial to HRH The Prince Consort, and is incorporated by Royal Charter.

Fencing lesson at Framlingham College.

Debenham Boys' School.

Eye National School, 1905. The school dates from 1858.

Boys feeding poultry at Eye Grammar School, 1915. From the sixteenth century the Guildhall was used as the school. In 1878 extensions to the school were built, and new buildings were added in 1911.

Bee-keeping at Eye Grammar School, 1915. The grammar school was one of the oldest scholastic foundations in the country. Twenty-two headmasters had been appointed before 1548.

Boys gardening at Eye Grammar School, 1915. The school obviously gave a good, all-round education, and these photographs are evidence that it included a sound rural education and did not concentrate upon turning country children into townspeople.

Girls gardening at Eye Grammar School, 1915. Girls were also taught cookery and laundry work. We can only applaud this school's many activities and regret that, against spirited local opposition, it ceased to be a grammar school in 1965.

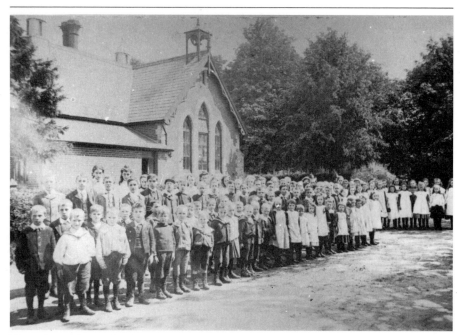

Thorndon Village School.

Hoxne School, *c.* 1913, endowed by Thomas Maynard of Hoxne Hall. The school was built on to the rear of the schoolmaster's house (now the doctor's surgery). A large (Victorian) school was built on Hackfield Green, then extended and rebuilt around 1914.

Fressingfield School, 1906–7. The headmaster, H.J. Joyce, is on the left. In 1685 'certain fee-farms should be charged with the payment of £10 per year to a schoolmaster for which he should teach five poor boys of the parish the three Rs and the Church Catechism and Creed'.

Laxfield Girls' Junior School. In her will (2 February 1721) Mrs Ann Ward directed that money from the income of her estate should be applied towards the education of poor boys and girls in Laxfield. The schoolmaster to receive £20 annually for teaching ten boys, the schoolmistress £10 for teaching ten girls.

Pupils at Badingham School, 1930s, before it became the village hall.

Dennington School, 1937.

Farming

The quiet of their strenuous farming days.

Adrian Bell

Red Polls on a Badingham farm. The breed is naturally hornless and noted for its docility, longevity and thriftiness. The best cows were good milkers and the steers made excellent beef.

As far as agriculture and the countryside are concerned, the true end of the Middle Ages is not the accession of the Tudors but the introduction of the internal combustion engine.

George Ewart Evans, 1960

From at least the sixteenth century central Suffolk was noted for its dairying, and its dairy cows were already a distinct regional breed. The district around Debenham had fairly large dairy herds which produced quantities of butter and cheese. By 1639 tumble-churns for butter making were in use at Fressingfield.

In the mid-seventeenth century central Suffolk was the first area in England to grow turnips as a field crop. By 1800 hemp was grown in quantity in the district between Eye and Beccles.

Mr Freeman of Aspall, near Debenham, was, if not the first driller on strong land in Suffolk, certainly among the very first.

Arthur Young, first Secretary to the Board of Agriculture, 1813

Most hedges at Badingham already existed in 1614. Enclosure of Suffolk, begun in the Middle Ages, was completed by Parliamentary Acts during the nineteenth century. By 1870 Hindes Groom blamed 'high farming' for making 'one huge field' out of five or six, and for 'swallowing most of the smaller holdings'.

The Framlingham and District Agricultural Co-operative Society was formed in 1903, and within four years it was the largest of its kind in England.

The first tractor appeared in Suffolk during the First World War.

Laying tile drains at Laxfield. In order to grow crops successfully on heavy clay soil, drainage was essential. Before the introduction of hollow-draining, land was surface drained. At first brushwood or straw was used for hollow-drainage. Tile draining was recorded in 1817.

Dung carting at Laxfield. The tumbrils could be tipped in stages to facilitate removal of the dung, which was put in regularly spaced heaps across the field and later spread. Unlike the ubiquitous and obnoxious slurry of today, this farmyard manure had the sweet smell of fertility.

Ploughing at Laxfield, *c.* 1890. This is an early type of plough, the AY, with a single stilt.

Ploughing at Badingham. Ransomes of Ipswich was making this type of iron plough, the YL, by 1844.

Ploughing at Badingham with Suffolk Horses. The fields were ploughed in stetches (lanes) leaving open furrows to help drainage. The distance between stetches was narrower if the field was a very wet one.

Drilling corn in the spring at Laxfield. The drill is a steerage drill made by James Smyth and Sons of Peasenhall, who started making corn drills in 1800. Drilling corn, as opposed to broadcasting or dibbling, was established in Suffolk by 1803. Hiring drills was the usual practice for many years, but by 1900 most Suffolk farmers had their own drills.

Nonpareil Corn Drills

FOR HORSE AND TRACTOR WORK

Also BEET SEED AND ROOT DRILLS with independent or fixed rolls   Over 32,000 Drills sold

JAMES SMYTH & SONS LIMITED

Corn and Seed Drill Makers and Ironfounders

Advertisement for Smyth's Nonpareil Drill. These drills, introduced in 1860, were very accurate and Smyth's made them for about 100 years. It is a swing-drill, which enabled it to make straight parallel lines across the field. The Nonpareil was exported to the continent, the Colonies, America, and Russia.

Horse-hoeing corn at Laxfield. The hoeing of corn dates from the early nineteenth century. Straight parallel lines were a great help when hoeing this way.

Harvesting at Badingham. The earlier type of horse-drawn reapers left the sheaves unbound. Here a reaper-binder is being used, which bound the sheaves with twine. It was hard work for the horses, who pulled the machine, driven by the land-wheel, round the field in an anti-clockwise direction. Incidentally, it's a good crop of wheat.

Sheaves and shocks, Badingham. In the foreground the sheaves of wheat as thrown from the binder (which would have been travelling away from the camera). On the right are shocks (stooks) made by the men who worked in the opposite direction. 'Ten sheaves to a stook is the best number' was a decision made by the Framlingham Farmers' Club in July 1840.

Harvest scene at Framlingham. The binder was eventually replaced by the combine harvester during the 1950s, which also replaced the threshing machine.

A much older method of reaping – harvesting with scythes at Debenham. The men are sharpening the scythes with Carborundum stones, and the man on the left has a cradle on his scythe to catch the crop as it is cut.

The last load of the harvest at Crows Hall, Debenham, *c.* 1900. This shows how the work was done in the days before machinery: the muscle and sweat of many men and horses, but not, apparently, of the farmer and his son on the right.

Harvest at Glebe Farm, Dennington, 1927. Standing far right is Mr Bridges, head horseman, and next to him is George Taylor.

A Morphy, Morphodite or Hermaphrodite. The rear end (left) is a tumbril, with its shafts fixed to a cross-member and connected to the axle of the smaller wheels in front, complete with shafts. Thus a tumbril could be converted into a wagon at haysel and harvest.

Thatching a corn stack at Laxfield. The small cart (centre) contains water to dampen the thatching straw. The horse rake (right) gathers the loose remnants of the crop after the sheaves have been carried.

Corn stacks at Badingham. These trim stacks, neatly thatched and safe from the weather, illustrate what skill, what an eye for form those workers had, combining beauty with utility.

Threshing at Badingham. This photograph shows the steam engine, threshing machine, elevator to take the threshed straw to the straw stack, horse and tumbril to haul the sacks of corn. The women have probably brought refreshment, providing a welcome break to this dusty, laborious job.

Drilling at Badingham, with a Smyth drill and Fordson Major Tractor, 1953. In one parish, a hundred years earlier, 65 acres were hand-dibbled. Three holes to the foot, three grains to a hole, making a total of 11 million holes.

A field at Badingham. It is early spring, the trees are still bare as is the ground. Each woman has a basket and what looks like a stick. What are they doing? One suggestion is stone picking, but could they be planting something, or weeding?

Geoffrey Hurran and his son, Fred, horse-hoeing roots at Fressingfield, a job that entailed a lot of walking and some concentration. 'Lead the horse as slowly as foot can fall', was the advice. Note the windmill in the background.

Hand-hoeing sugar beet at Low Farm, Laxfield. A tedious and·back-breaking job – how they must have welcomed the photographer. But not a lonely job and they could talk and joke as they worked. A sugar-beet factory was established at Lavenham in 1869, but few farmers would grow the crop and the factory closed four years later. The crop only became popular after the Sugar Beet Subsidy Act of 1925.

Bringing in the soft fruit. Noah Thirkettle's farm at Wells Corner, Laxfield, around 1906.

A vixen and her cubs, caught and killed in Laxfield.

Suffolk Horses at Dennington, early twentieth century. The Suffolk Horse is said to have existed in the sixteenth century. 'The Suffolk breed of horses, is no less celebrated than the cows. They are found in most perfection . . . in the district extending to Woodbridge, Debenham, Eye and Lowestoft', Arthur Young, 1813. The first *Suffolk Stud Book* was started in 1880 by Herman Biddell, who traced all the horses then alive, which were all pedigree horses descended from Mr Crisp's horse at Ufford, born in 1768. Clean hocks, a superior stamina, and pulling power made it a popular breed. It is believed that the Suffolk was the only horse that would pull twice at a dead weight. Before 1880 many small farmers had valuable Suffolk mares, but hard times forced them to sell to wealthy breeders and fill their own stables with inferior types. Suffolks were exported to Canada, the USA and New Zealand. The breed reached its peak in 1919, but numbers had declined drastically by the mid-1950s.

Suffolk horsemen and Suffolk Horse standing by a horse-pool at Badingham.

George Kerridge with a Suffolk stallion, Debenham, *c.* 1938. During the mating season Mr Kerridge travelled the district with a Suffolk stallion.

Red Poll bull, bred at Laxfield. The Red Poll is the result of merging two breeds, the Suffolk Dun and the Norfolk. Arthur Young spoke highly of the milking abilities of the Suffolk Dun, which he called 'the little mongrel breed'. 'These Suffolk cows have been long celebrated for their great quantity of milk . . . There are few dairies of any consideration ·in the district that do not contain cows which give . . . eight gallons of milk in the day; and six or more are not uncommon . . . For two or three months a whole dairy will give five gallons a day on average.' By 1846 the merging of the two breeds was complete and the dual-purpose Red Poll was the result. In 1874 the first *Herd Book* was published, and a Red Poll Cattle Society formed in 1888. The breed found favour in East Anglia and gradually spread to all parts of Britain, and many parts of the world. By 1949 there were 600 registered herds in Britain. By the early 1950s the Red Poll had reached its zenith, but within a decade began to decline in numbers. During the last dozen years the decline has been drastic, with only a handful of milking herds left, and the sight of Red Polls in Suffolk is a rarity. A sad state for a breed with so much to commend it.

Red Polls at Aspall Hall, 1910. These animals, bred by J.B. Chevallier, won prizes at the London Dairy Show.

Wenhaston Dawn 10, 1955. A Red Poll cow bred by W.E. Smith at Tithe Farm, Fressingfield. It came first at the Royal Show 1954, was champion at the Essex Show 1955, and first at the Glasgow Dairy Show 1955, when she gave 8½ gallons in one day.

Suffolk sheep in a lambing pen at Laxfield. Sheep were an integral part of the Norfolk Four Course Rotation and were folded on fields of turnips and swedes. To find suitable sheep for the system the Norfolk Horn was crossed with the Southdown rams and from this evolved the Suffolk breed. It became a recognized breed by the late 1850s and the Suffolk Sheep Society was formed in 1886. The Suffolks became a very popular breed in this country and have been exported to many countries overseas. They are still the most popular breed of British sheep and the rams are used extensively for crossing with other breeds.

Suffolk sheep, Laxfield. 'Curly' Will Read was shepherd for Harry Davy, who farmed Street Farm, Yew Tree Farm, St Jacob's Farm and Dowsing Farm. Will Read lived in Church Walk, Laxfield.

Silvanus Bridges went to Framlingham around 1720 and started work as a wheelwright. Ledgers dating back to 1820 still exist and give details of the work of his great-grandchildren, Silvanus and John Fruer Bridges, who had blacksmith shops in Double Street and Fairfield Road. In this century the work was ironmongery and agricultural engineering, but a blacksmith was employed until the late 1950s. Then Charles Garrard's ironmongery business was acquired and the firm of Bridges and Garrard is now in Market Hill. The advertisement is from *Lamberts Almanac*, 1913.

SECTION TEN

People

Born of the East Wind.

H. Rider Haggard

The Framlingham Old Volunteers Band, during the procession at Framlingham, 1905.

Population	1801	1901	1931
Badingham	607	558	490
Debenham	1215	1182	1016
Dennington	726	625	535
Eye	1734	2004	1733
Framlingham	1856	2526	2101
Fressingfield	1044	1005	881
Horham	394	287	246
Hoxne	972	838	744
Laxfield	1008	827	736
Peasenhall	532	698	643
Stradbroke	1215	1016	903

Stradbroke sent about two hundred paupers to America between 1830 and 1844. In May 1836 about a hundred men, women and children were brought from north Suffolk by cart and wagon and embarked for Canada at Wherstead, watched by the Guardians of Hoxne Union.

In most rural parishes the population increased until the mid-nineteenth century, although it probably never attained that of the fourteenth century. It then began to decline and the rural exodus was accelerated after 1879 by the prolonged agricultural depression. In 1901 the Rural District Council of Hoxne lamented the loss of a quarter of its population in only forty years. The above table shows that the population of all the parishes continued to decline in numbers.

Handbell ringers, Fressingfield, 1900.

Handbell ringers, Stradbroke, 1920s.

Hoxne Band, *c.* 1912. Alex Copping (in uniform), playing the flute, was the first Hoxne soldier to be killed in the First World War. (Photograph by M.L. Rogers of Low Street)

Debenham Band, 1912.

John Perkins, head gardener at Thornham Hall, the residence of Lord Henniker, *c.* 1866. Between 1840 and 1850 John Perkins raised the Lady Henniker apple from one of the seedlings grown from seeds of the apples used for cider making. This particular tree was preserved and introduced in 1873, gaining a First Class Certificate from the Royal Horticultural Society. It is a dessert and culinary apple with a good flavour, and is still obtainable from some nurseries. (Photograph from the Cleer S. Alger Trust Collection)

The wedding of Alfred Tye, 15/19 Kings Hussars, and Miss Olive Gilman, both of Hoxne, 1930. The Tye and Gilman families are two of the oldest Hoxne families.

St Mary's church, Debenham.
Wedding of Miss Moore of Crows
Hall, Debenham, to Sydney Turner of
Mickfield.

Wedding group at Debenham.

Girls dancing at Dennington, *c.* 1910.

Stradbroke Fancy Fair.

Dennington Sunday school outing to Aldeburgh, 1913. The village pump is on the left. At Stone Hill, Badingham, some of the children had to get off and walk before the steam-engine lorry (by the pump) could get up the hill.

List's charabanc taking Debenham men to Clacton, 24 July 1926.

A meeting of the Eye Coursing Club at Haven Farm.

Hoxne Quoits Club at St Edmunds Hall Reading Room, built by Sir E.C. Kerrison, second baronet. A statue of St Edmund, reputed to have been killed at Hoxne, stands at the top of the front elevation.

Debenham Sports Committee, 1911.

Eye Flower Show Committee, 1930s.

The Earl and Countess of Stradbroke arriving for a hunt on Middleton Moor.

The Earl and Countess of Stradbroke at a hunt.

The new post office in Riverside, Framlingham, on Pension Day, 1 January 1909. This was the first day that pensions were paid due to the Old Age Pension Act. Everyone aged 70 or over was paid 5s. The cloak worn by the man on the right shows that he lived in the Hitcham's Almshouses. These almshouses were founded by Sir Robert Hitcham for six men and six women. The men received a cloak each year and the women a dress. John Self, tailor of Well Close, used to make the cloaks.

Drawing water at Debenham.

The Revd E. Cooke, vicar of Peasenhall, with his family, *c.* 1902. Apart from a 'little knot' of three or four, Mr Cooke believed that his parishioners led unblemished lives.

Three men of Dennington around the turn of the century. Left to right: Ted Briggs, Bob Reeve, Sam Marjoram. Their total ages amounted to 265 years.

Some more men of Dennington and of Framlingham. On the extreme right is Percy Frederick Allen, a well-known Framlingham butcher who had a shop in Bridge Street.

Debenham chimney sweep Marty Miller, his wife and three children. When he was a boy, Mr Miller was sent up chimneys to sweep them.

Badingham chimney sweep.

Rose Harsent (standing) of Peasenhall. The other woman is believed to be her half-sister, *c.* 1901. Rose Harsent was employed at Providence House where she lived-in. In June 1902 her father went to visit Rose early one Sunday morning and found her lying in the kitchen, dead and almost naked, surrounded by a pool of blood. She was 23 years of age. Dr Lay, who lived across the road, saw that her throat had been cut and estimated that she had been dead for about five hours. Several unsigned love letters were found in her room and one letter signed by William Gardiner.

William Gardiner, who lived in a cottage in Peasenhall Street with his wife and children, was a wheelwright at the Drill Works and a prominent Nonconformist in the district. Previously there had been gossip about his relations with Rose Harsent. He was arrested and tried twice for the murder. At the first trial, eleven members of the jury found him guilty, at the second trial eleven of the jury found him innocent. He was discharged and he and his family moved from Peasenhall.

Rose Harsent's father at his daughter's grave (see *The Peasenhall Murder* by Martin Fido and Keith Skinner, Alan Sutton, 1990).

Mr Holmes, a farmworker of Eye, *c.* 1880.

Edward Fisk, a shepherd of Laxfield.

Landgirls and farm men at Badingham, 1940s.

Army bakers at Framlingham during the First World War. In the Second World War the 390th Bombardment Group of the 8th American Army Air Force flew 300 missions and dropped 19,000 tons of bombs from the airfield at Framlingham. A total of 176 men from the base died on active service.

Women of the Red Cross, Fressingfield vicarage, 1917.

Bob Scoggins of Dennington, home on leave during the First World War.

Unveiling the First World War Memorial at Stradbroke.

Fressingfield Home Guard during the Second World War.

Miss Chevallier with a Red Poll cow at Aspall.

W.E. Smith with the Prize Cup being congratulated by Princess Alexandra at the Suffolk Agricultural Show. His son, Norman, is on the left. Mr Smith of Fressingfield won many prizes with his Wenhaston herd of Red Polls. He started breeding them at Wenhaston, hence his herd prefix. He also bred Suffolk Horses and Long White Lop Ear pigs.

The Taylor family, Dennington.

Dennington Women's Institute outing to Yarmouth, 1943. The Dennington Women's Institute was formed in 1922.

A shoot at Brome Hall with Mr Hill-Wood, who was a relative of Lady Bateman of Brome Hall (the sister of Sir Edward Kerrison).

Outdoor theatricals at Dennington, *c.* 1900. Left back: John Studd. Right: Archie Baldry. Centre: Bob Reeve. Archie Baldry was the last member of the Baldry family to own the post office at Dennington.

Badingham postmen. How many
people can remember these postmen's
hats?

Mr Pepper, postman at Badingham,
1950s.

The Jolly family with their caravan at Denham Green, Hoxne. Several generations of the family were thatchers in the district.

Princess Victoria Mary on a visit to Dennington while staying with Lord and Lady Stradbroke at Henham Hall, 31 October 1906.

Mr Mayhew, Dr Biden's groom, Laxfield.

Workers at the drill works, Peasenhall, with a soldier friend. Does he date the photograph to between 1914 and 1918?

Men of Peasenhall, *c.* 1915. Dr Lay is wearing a panama hat and on his left is the Revd E. Cooke wearing a boater.

Mr Arthur Daines, basketmaker, by the
village pump at Dennington, 1921.

A smart turn-out at Framlingham.

Theatricals at Fressingfield School, *c.* 1922.

Stradbroke Amateur Dramatic Club, 1929, in a performance of *Come Out of the Kitchen.*

Debenham faces, *c*. 1938. George Kerridge and friend.

Acknowledgements

Badingham Women's Institute • Mr D. Banthorpe • Mr J. Bridges
Cleer S. Alger Trust • Mrs Daines • Mr S. Evans • Mr S. Govier
Lanman Museum • Laxfield Museum • Miss F. Legg • Mr D. Moyse
Mr D. Neave • Mrs Perry • Mr H. Plant • Mrs Poppy • Mr N. Smith
Revd David Streeter • Mr N. Walker • Mr R. Wardley • Mr H. Woods